AMERICAN
HUMANE

Protecting Children & Animals Since 1877

Beginning Pet Care
WITH AMERICAN HUMANE

Learning to Care for SMALL MAMMALS

Bailey Books
an imprint of
Enslow Publishers, Inc.
40 Industrial Road
Box 398
Berkeley Heights, NJ 07922
USA
http://www.enslow.com

Felicia Lowenstein Niven

AMERICAN HUMANE

Protecting Children & Animals Since 1877

Founded in 1877, the American Humane Association is the only national organization dedicated to protecting both children and animals. Through a network of child and animal protection agencies and individuals, American Humane develops policies, legislation, curricula, and training programs — and takes action — to protect children and animals from abuse, neglect, and exploitation. To learn how you can support American Humane's vision of a nation where no child or animal will ever be a victim of abuse or neglect, visit www.americanhumane. org, phone (303) 792-9900, or write to the American Humane Association at 63 Inverness Drive East, Englewood, Colorado, 80112-5117.

To our Readers:

We have done our best to make sure all Internet Addresses in this book were active and appropriate when we went to press. However, the author and the publisher have no control over and assume no liability for the material available on those Internet sites or on other Web sites they may link to. Any comments or suggestions can be sent by e-mail to comments@enslow.com or to the address on the back cover.

Every effort has been made to locate all copyright holders of material used in this book. If any errors or omissions have occurred, corrections will be made in future editions of this book.

For my dear friend Sharon, who introduced me to an extraordinary rabbit named Oatis.

Bailey Books, an imprint of Enslow Publishers, Inc.

Copyright © 2011 by Enslow Publishers, Inc.

Library of Congress Cataloging-in-Publication Data

Niven, Felicia Lowenstein.
  Learning to care for small mammals / Felicia Lowenstein Niven.
    p. cm. — (Beginning pet care with American Humane)
  Includes bibliographical references and index.
  Summary: "Readers will learn how to choose and care for small mammals"—Provided by publisher.
  ISBN 978-0-7660-3195-1
  1. Rabbits—Juvenile literature. 2. Rodents as pets—Juvenile literature. 3. Ferrets as pets—Juvenile literature. I. Title.
  SF453.2.N58 2011
  636.935—dc22

                                   2009026191

Printed in China

052010 Leo Paper Group, Heshan City, Guangdong, China

10 9 8 7 6 5 4 3 2 1

Illustration Credits: All animals in logo bar and boxes, Shutterstock. Carolyn A. McKeone/Photo Researchers, Inc., pp. 3 (thumbnail 4), 22, 23, 29, 30, 39, 43; © iStockphoto.com/Rosemarie Gearhart, p. 21; Jaaini, pp. 3 (thumbnail 1), 4, 7; Jörg Carstensen/dpa/Landov, pp. 3 (thumbnail 2), 12, 16; NYPL/Photo Researchers, Inc., p. 9; Shutterstock, pp. 1, 3 (thumbnails 5, 6), 10, 18, 24, 31, 32, 34, 36, 40–41; UWE ZUCCHI/dpa/Landov, pp. 3 (thumbnail 3), 15; www.petwerks.com, p. 26.

Cover Illustration: Shutterstock (tan and brown rabbit).

Table of Contents

Chapter 1

Rescue

Smuchers was rescued from a shelter.

The black-and-white bunny had a runny nose. Unlike the other bunnies, Smuchers was very still. He was breathing heavily. The only time he moved was when he sneezed.

The Hug-a-Bunny Shelter was the perfect place for him to get well. But it would take many months before he could be adopted.

Rescue

Jaaini saw Smuchers's picture on the shelter Web site. She had grown up with rabbits on her family's farm. She loved them! Also, Smuchers was very cute.

But Jaaini and her husband had just gotten a puppy. She knew that rabbits and dogs do not usually get along. She tried to forget about Smuchers.

That did not mean she stopped checking the Web site. After awhile, she saw that the rabbit's picture had disappeared. He had been adopted. Jaaini was happy for him, but sad that she could not take him home.

Then something happened. A few days later, Smuchers's picture was back. What had happened? Jaaini called the shelter.

Smuchers had stayed just two days with his new family. They discovered they were allergic to rabbits.

Now the shelter was being very careful about the family that would adopt Smuchers. The next home had to be his "forever" home.

5

Jaaini talked to her husband. There was the problem of the puppy. That could be solved by getting a nice large cage for Smuchers. They would also be careful never to let the dog and rabbit loose in the same room together until they were sure the animals got along well together—and then, only under close supervision.

Jaaini was convinced it would work. She called the shelter.

"I told them I had never given up a pet before," she said. "I knew how to care for a rabbit. I wanted him to have a long and happy life."

The shelter checked out Jaaini's home. They interviewed her. They also talked to her husband. Finally, they agreed to let her adopt Smuchers.

The day that Jaaini met Smuchers was filled with emotion. The shelter volunteer cried.

Jaaini and her family adopted Smuchers. He's now in a very good home.

Rescue

She had cared for the rabbit for a long time. Jaaini understood. She promised to keep in touch.

It took a few weeks for the rabbit to feel comfortable in his new home. Now he loves to run around the living room. He even jumps up on the couch. So far, the dog and the rabbit have only touched noses together—through the cage. That is as far as their friendship will go for now, until they spend more time getting used to each other, according to Jaaini.

"Smuchers is very special," she said. "He loves to be brushed. He likes being kissed on his nose and scratched on the top of his head. He really is a spunky boy and not a cuddly bun, and that's okay with us."

Chapter 2
History of Small Mammals

You would expect to see a rabbit in the woods. But a wild rabbit like that would not make a good pet. Neither would wild mice, rats, or other small mammals.

Do you know the story of Peter Rabbit? Beatrix Potter, the girl on the left, wrote the stories.

History of Small Mammals

The small mammals that we keep as pets come from a long line of domesticated animals. In many cases, they have been pets for thousands of years.

It probably started with mice. In China, people used mice in religious ceremonies. In Japan, they thought that mice were messengers from the gods. The Greeks thought that mice could predict the future.

People kept ferrets for a different reason. They were working pets. They helped hunt rabbits. They also helped control mice or rats.

Over the centuries, some of these animals became true pets. People spent time with them. They held and petted them. The pets became part of the family.

History of Small Mammals

Guinea pigs were introduced as pets in Europe in the early 1500s. Prettily colored mice and rats became pets in the 1800s. Rabbits were popular pets at that time, too. People who lived in cities kept rabbits to stay connected to the feeling of being in the country.

That is not to say that all small mammals became pets. Some stayed in the wild. The ones that grew up with people started to change. They became tame. They lost some of their wild traits. They passed that on to their children.

In the 1930s, hamsters were tamed and bred as pets. Gerbils were bred since the 1960s. During the past fifty years, rats, mice, guinea pigs, rabbits, and ferrets all became familiar household animals.

Today, many of these animals are popular choices for pets. They make wonderful friends for people of all ages.

Chapter 3

Getting a Small Mammal

Smuchers is a rabbit, but he is also a small mammal. Mammals are warm-blooded animals with hair or fur. Many mammals make good pets. They are clean and do not make much noise.

There are many different kinds of mammals that make good pets, too.

Before you bring your new pet home, make sure you have everything you need. Some animals need an area just for sleeping or for playing.

Getting a Small Mammal

There are rabbits, guinea pigs, gerbils, and hamsters. There are rats, mice, and ferrets. If you do your research, you can find the right one for your family.

Rabbits

Rabbits might be a good choice for a family pet. They can weigh as little as two pounds or as much as sixteen pounds. Pet rabbits live about eight to twelve years.

How Big Is Big Enough?

What size cage should you get? For the active ferret, you need a large cage with two or three levels. Rabbits need a cage that is at least four times as long as their body. The tinier gerbil or hamster needs less space.

You can find cages made especially for your type of small mammal at most pet stores. Remember to add more space if you get more than one animal.

Getting a Small Mammal

Rabbits need to live indoors in a cage where it is not too hot or too cold. They also need to spend a few hours outside of their cage every day so that they can exercise. You need to clean the cage each day. That can be a lot of work.

Some people are allergic to rabbit fur. Others are allergic to the hay that rabbits need to eat. Rabbits would not be a good choice for these people.

Guinea pigs

Guinea pigs, or cavies, are about five inches tall and weigh about thirty-five ounces. Some have short hair. Others have long hair. Pet guinea pigs live for about five to seven years.

Guinea pigs are awake during the day and sleep at night. That makes them a good choice for a pet.

Guinea pigs live in cages. They need a certain temperature, 65 to 75 degrees Fahrenheit.

Guinea pigs are active during the day. Some small mammals are active at night.

Getting a Small Mammal

They need a place to hide, such as a small box. You can also buy a house or igloo made especially for them at your local pet store.

Gerbils or Hamsters

Gerbils and hamsters are relatives of rats and mice. Gerbils have tails. Hamsters do not.

Believe it or not, rats can make good pets!

Getting a Small Mammal

Gerbils weigh two to three ounces. Hamsters weigh six to seven ounces. Hamsters and gerbils live two to four years.

Gerbils can be awake during the day and night. Hamsters are nocturnal. Nocturnal means they are awake during the night. They sleep during the day. Hamsters might keep you up at night with their movement. They might be asleep when you want to play.

Rats and Mice

Rats and mice are also nocturnal. They are relatives of gerbils and hamsters. They live two to four years.

Rats weigh about sixteen ounces. They measure about ten inches long without their tails. Mice weigh about one ounce. They are about three inches without the tail.

Getting a Small Mammal

Ferrets are very active pets. Before you choose a ferret as a pet, make sure ferrets are allowed in your state.

Rats are very intelligent and social. They usually do not mind being handled.

Ferrets

Ferrets are very active and playful pets. They come in a lot of colors. Ferrets can weigh up to four and a half pounds. They live for about six to eight years.

Ferrets have a strong smell that comes from the musk oils in their skin. This smell may bother some people. They also need to spend several hours a day outside of their cage to exercise.

Getting a Small Mammal

Ferrets are also very social and are happier when they have at least one other ferret to play with. Ferrets need to get yearly vaccinations for rabies and distemper.

Not all states or cities allow pet ferrets. You cannot have a ferret in California, Hawaii, or New York City. Other places make you get a license. Check with your local fish and game or wildlife department for the rules.

Making the Decision

The Walt Disney movie *Bedtime Stories* has a furry star. It is a guinea pig named Bugsy. At first, the script called for a hamster. But hamsters do not like to be handled that much. Guinea pigs do. The director decided to switch the type of animal. It worked well.

Figure out what is most important to you. Do you want an animal that likes to be held?

Getting a Small Mammal

Do you want to play with your pet after school? Do you need an animal that fits into a smaller space? Are you ready for an animal that needs a lot of care?

Where can you get a small mammal? The best place is at your local animal shelter. If your shelter does not have the kind of small mammal you are looking for, ask for the name of a rescue group. These groups usually charge a small fee just to cover their costs.

Some pet shops also sell small mammals. Sometimes the animals at pet shops are treated well, but sometimes they are not. Wherever you go to get your pet, pay attention to the surroundings and the animals. Is the place clean? Do the animals look healthy? Ask a lot of questions. Make sure you are getting a healthy pet.

Remember that some of these animals are nocturnal. You might want to see them as close to evening as you can. Otherwise, they could be asleep.

Getting a Small Mammal

Make an appointment with a veterinarian as soon as you can. On the first visit, the vet will examine your pet. Best of all, the vet can answer your questions. Write them down so you do not forget what you want to know.

Small mammals make great pets!

Chapter 4
Health and Exercise

You are ready to bring your new pet home! Do you have everything you need?

In addition to a cage, rabbits and ferrets need a litter box. Place the box in the cage with your pet, but away from where he sleeps. You should also provide a litter box for your pet when you take him out of the cage.

Health and Exercise

All of your pets need fresh water every day. This ferret drinks from a special water bottle.

Put a few droppings in the box. That will give your pet the idea that he should use the box as his bathroom.

For both pets, you will need to use a type of litter that is safe. Clumping types of cat litter are not good for rabbits or ferrets. Cedar, pine, and clay litters also are not good for rabbits. Rabbits may even eat their litter! The best choice for them is a litter made from paper or wood pulp.

Your new pet will also need fresh food every day.

Health and Exercise

Your pet also needs food and water. You might use a water bottle that hangs on the cage. This is a good choice. If you use dishes for ferrets and rabbits, find weighted ones. Ferrets and rabbits like to knock them over.

You will need to find the right food for your pet. For example, rabbits need to eat a very specific diet of rabbit pellets, timothy grass hay, and fresh vegetables. Feeding them the wrong types of foods can make them sick. Carrots and parsley are good. Tomato leaves and vines can be poisonous.

You can find the right food at pet stores. Remember if your pet is nocturnal, the best time to feed him is at night.

Do you need a brush? Most small mammals groom themselves. But long-haired rabbits and guinea pigs need to be brushed every day or their fur will become matted.

Rabbits need a special place to live called a hutch.

You may need to trim your pet's nails. Ferrets', rabbits', and guinea pigs' nails grow quickly and need to be trimmed every few weeks. Rats, mice, gerbils, and hamsters usually wear down their nails by their active play.

It is important to wash your hands before and after you touch your pet—each and every time! This will keep you, and her, safe from spreading germs.

26

Health and Exercise

Exercise will also keep your pet healthy. Hamsters, gerbils, rats, and mice can exercise right in their cages. Give them tubes to crawl through, wheels to spin, and places to climb. Empty cardboard tissue boxes or paper towel rolls make great hiding places for hamsters and gerbils.

Some animals need more space to exercise. Ferrets and rabbits need two to four hours outside their cage every day to remain healthy. They like to run, jump, twist in the air, and bump into objects. Just make sure to watch your pet closely.

You have given a loving home to a pet. Not all pets are so lucky. There are many homeless pets in the world. This problem is called pet overpopulation. That is why many people choose to spay or neuter their pets.

Spaying and neutering are operations that prevent animals from having babies. It is called spaying

fast facts

It is important to wash your hands before and after you touch your pet—each and every time! This will keep you, and her, safe from spreading germs.

for a female and neutering for a male. Your veterinarian does these operations.

Not all small mammals are spayed or neutered. But it is recommended for certain ones, including rabbits, guinea pigs, and ferrets. Spaying or neutering your pet can make her healthier by preventing some types of diseases. For example, female ferrets and rabbits that are not spayed can get sick and even die.

Importantly, talk to your vet. Schedule yearly visits so she can check your pet. This will help keep him healthy.

Bring your new pet to a vet right away. It's helpful to have a list of questions ready!

Chapter 5

Problems and Challenges

Be sure to check on your pet every day to see that he is eating and drinking.

Ferrets have been known to untwist bottle caps. They can unzip zippers with their front paws, too. They can squeeze in tiny openings. You can imagine that they could get into plenty of trouble.

And it is not just ferrets. Rabbits love to chew on electrical cords.

Rats have teeth that keep growing. Special wooden blocks can help wear down the teeth.

So do rats. You will need to pet-proof your house.

Make sure dangerous materials are out of reach. A pet could chew or swallow wires, paper clips, pins, staples, and rubber bands. Even some houseplants are poisonous.

You will also want to protect your pet against health problems. Here are some common ones.

Overgrown Teeth

Some animals have teeth that keep growing. These include gerbils, mice, rats, and rabbits. They constantly chew on things to keep their teeth trimmed. You can give them wooden blocks to chew on.

However, sometimes the teeth do not line up in the right way. Chewing does not wear them down. In these cases, you will have to get your pet's teeth clipped. If you let them

Your small mammal may like to be handled. He may even climb on your shoulder!

grow, your pet will not be able to eat. He can have more dental problems.

Skin Problems

Skin problems are common in many small mammals. You might notice them because of hair loss. This is different from shedding. Your pet will have bare patches.

Many skin problems are caused by parasites. These are tiny creatures that feed on your pet. Fleas, mites, and lice are just some examples. They can cause your pet to itch. Your pet may look tired. Most parasites can be treated with medicine.

Respiratory Problems

You know how awful you feel when you have a cold. Your nose is stopped up. You have a respiratory problem. The word respiratory means "breathing."

Giving your rabbit fresh vegetables is good for him. Always ask your vet which is the best food for your small mammal.

Animals get sick that way, too. But when that happens, it is usually more serious than a cold. They can get infections, even pneumonia.

You will know if your pet is sick. He may sniffle or sneeze. There may be stuff coming out of his nose. If your pet is having trouble breathing, see your vet right away.

Digestive Problems

Sometimes pets have digestive problems. Digestion is what happens to food in our bodies after we eat it.

Make sure you always feed your pet the right food. A rabbit's whole digestive tract can stop working if he is fed the wrong diet. Make sure that you feed your rabbit lots of timothy grass hay every day plus pellets and some fresh vegetables. The hay contains fiber that will keep him healthy.

Do not overfeed him or give too many treats. Just like people, small mammals can become fat, and this can lead to a lot of health problems.

Those are some of the health problems. You may also find some concerns with behavior. Here are some common ones.

35

Spending time with your small mammal will help you bond with him.

Problems and Challenges

Biting

Biting is part of the natural behavior of many small mammals. Ferrets, for example, bite as part of play. If your ferret nips at you, put her back in her cage. Wait a little while. Then take her out again. Repeat this until your ferret learns not to bite you.

Rabbits, rats, and guinea pigs do not usually bite. Mice and hamsters, however, might nip at you. They bite because they are afraid.

If you have a mouse or hamster that bites, you will need to build her trust. Spend time near her cage and talk to her. Do not try to touch her. After a few days, put your hand just inside the top of the cage. Each day, you can go a little farther. You can let her sniff your hand if she becomes curious. Finally, try giving her a small bit of raisin or apple from your hand.

Once she takes the treats, you can try to pick her up. Remember to gently cup her in your hand.

Males and Females

Many small mammals are social. That means they like to be with friends. But be careful. Some animals will fight with each other. This happens a lot with male animals. Unless they have been raised together, do not put two males in the same cage.

But it does not happen just with males. Female rabbits usually do not get along with each other. If you want more than one rabbit, it is best to pair a neutered male with a spayed female.

Sometimes females of other species also fight. You will need to watch them carefully to make sure they are getting along.

Finally, there are animals that like to be alone. Some breeds of hamsters are solitary. They cannot be kept in the same cage with other hamsters.

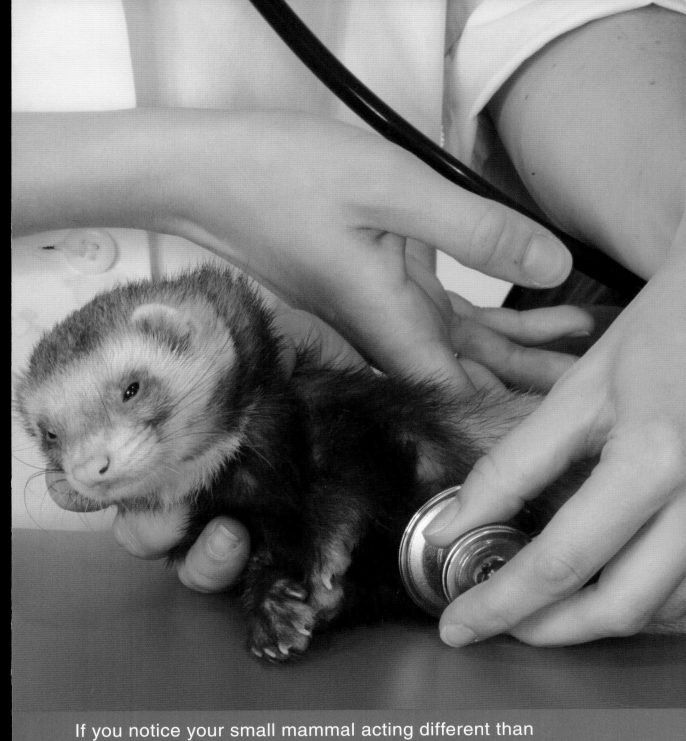

If you notice your small mammal acting different than usual, call your vet right away.

Chapter 6

A Lifelong Responsibility

Pets may help us laugh!

Beauregard was a very lucky rat. Because he was sick, he was almost sold as food for a snake. But a kind pet store employee saved his life. Jelena Woehr brought him home. She nursed him to health. She taught him to trust her.

Now Beauregard follows her around like a puppy. He bosses her dog around.

A Lifelong Responsibility

He knows his name. He has learned to walk on his hind legs for a treat. Once, he leapt into her cereal bowl. He fished out a piece of cereal covered in milk. He enjoyed his treat while hiding under the couch.

Beauregard is Jelena's for as long as he lives. That is because the pet you bring home is your responsibility. He will probably share your life for many years. In return for food, shelter, and medical care, he will give you so much.

Animals can improve our mood. They can keep us from feeling lonely. They are always there to happily greet us. They entertain us when they play. They can even be good listeners. In these ways, they reduce stress. They help to make us happier people.

You can share a strong bond with your small mammal. It is every bit as strong as with a dog or cat.

A Lifelong Responsibility

Millions of people have discovered that fact. Clint Eastwood, a famous actor in Westerns, has a rabbit. *High School Musical*'s Vanessa Anne Hudgens owns a bunny, too.

You do not have to be famous to give a small mammal a good home. Simply spend the time to care for your pet. Make a difference in his life and you will have a loyal friend.

Your pet hamster can be a good friend.

Glossary

animal shelter—An organization that cares for homeless pets.

behavior—The actions of an animal.

mammal—A warm-blooded animal with hair or fur that nurses its young.

neuter—To perform an operation on a male animal to prevent babies.

nocturnal—Sleeping during the day and awake at night.

parasites—Organisms that feed on other animals.

rescue group—A group that finds homes for needy and homeless animals.

shedding—A natural process where hair falls out.

solitary—Being alone.

spay—To perform an operation on a female animal to prevent babies.

trait—Something that is typical of a certain type of animal; a characteristic.

vaccine—A shot to prevent disease.

veterinarian ("vet") —A doctor specializing in animals.

warm-blooded—Having a steady body temperature, even if the environment is a different temperature.

Further Reading

Books

Doudna, Kelly. *Frisky Ferrets*. Edina, Minn.:
ABDO Pub. Co., 2007.

Foran, Jill. *Caring for Your Hamster*. Mankato,
Minn.: Weigl, 2003.

Johnson, Jinny. *Rabbits*. Mankato, Minn.: Black
Rabbit Books, 2009.

Loves, June. *Mice and Rats*. Philadelphia:
Chelsea Clubhouse, 2004.

Newcomb, Rain, and Rose McLarney. *Is My
Hamster Wild? The Secret Lives of
Hamsters, Gerbils & Guinea Pigs*
Asheville, N.C.: Lark Books, 2008.

Further Reading

Internet Addresses

American Humane Association
   <http://www.americanhumane.org>

ASPCA Animaland for Kids
   <http://www.animaland.org>

Index